RACEWAYS

Other Boston Children's Museum Activity Books
by Bernie Zubrowski:

Ball-Point Pens
Bubbles
Messing Around with Baking Chemistry
Messing Around with Drinking Straws
Messing Around with Water Pumps
Milk Carton Blocks

RACEWAYS

Having Fun with Balls and Tracks

by Bernie Zubrowski
illustrated by Roy Doty

A Boston Children's Museum Activity Book

William Morrow and Company • New York

To the children of the Vietnamese and Cambodian refugees who have recently come to this country

The author would like to thank Gary Goldstein of Tufts University for checking the accuracy of the scientific explanations in this book.

Text copyright © 1985 by Bernard Zubrowski and The Children's Museum, Boston
Illustrations copyright © 1985 by Roy Doty

Library of Congress Cataloging in Publication Data
Zubrowski, Bernie.   Raceways: having fun with balls and tracks   (A Boston Children's Museum activity book). Summary: Presents a selection of games to be played or made with balls and tracks. Illustrates some scientific principles such as gravity, momentum, and kinetic energy. 1. Ball games—Juvenile literature. 2. Games—Juvenile literature. [1. Ball games. 2. Games. 3. Scientific recreations] I. Doty, Roy, 1922– ill. II. Title. III. Series.   GV861.Z82 1985   796.3   84-20600
ISBN 0-688-04159-0/ISBN 0-688-04160-4 (pbk.)

Contents

Introduction

If you drop a ball from a certain height, it will always fall straight down. When you roll a ball across the floor, it will go in a straight line unless it hits a bump. When you roll a ball along a track, it can move in different ways depending on how you have arranged the track.

Rolling balls down tracks has been a favorite pastime of children for a long time. It is fun to create different-shaped pathways, and it is exciting to watch how the balls move on them.

This book shows you several types of games you can make with balls and tracks. Some have been popular for a long time, others are new. Most don't require much equipment to assemble. You will learn how to make a ball go up and down hills, travel in a circle, and jump from track to track without falling off.

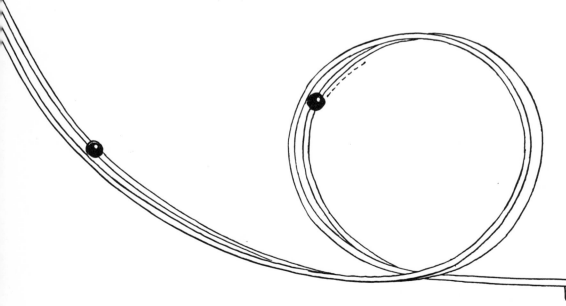

When you do the various games and experiments in this book, you can start from the beginning and do each one in sequence. Or you can drop in here and there, trying those you find most interesting. Each game also has different levels of challenges. The "Further Challenges" sections are the most difficult. For some you will have to be careful and patient in putting them together. The last section on Rube Goldberg machines should be attempted only after you have done several of the simple games first. It will give you more experience and also lots of ideas for creating devices of your own.

What you may not realize when playing with balls and tracks is that you can learn some science at the same time. By asking the right kinds of questions and experimenting with the devices you make, you can learn about such scientific ideas as energy, acceleration, and momentum. If you watch carefully how balls move down tracks, you can begin to understand how many other things move, too.

Getting Started

You don't need many things to make most of the games and devices in this book. You may already have some in your house.

ASSEMBLING THE TRACK

To make the track, you will need:

> 4 or 5 pieces of plastic molding, each about 244 cm.
> (8 ft.) long
> broom holders
> pieces of wood, about 20 cm. (8 in.) long, and screws
> 9 cm. ($3\frac{1}{2}$ in.) wide

The most important material is the molding. The kind you will need is decorative molding. This is available in paneling supply stores. It is used to finish off the edges and corners of paneled rooms. Molding is made of wood or plastic and comes in different shapes. You will need the plastic molding, either cove or inside-corner shaped. Test it to make sure it bends easily, because you will have to bend it into all kinds of shapes for these games. Some plastic is too rigid.

The shape of the molding is also important. Here are two kinds that work best for rolling balls:

ACTUAL SIZE

The first kind, *A*, will work for most of the arrangements suggested in the book. The second kind, *B*, is a little more expensive; but because the sides are higher, it will keep the rolling balls on the track better, especially when they are moving very quickly.

Before you buy the molding, check that there are no bends, twists, or bumps in it. Otherwise, your balls will not roll properly.

When laying down your track, make sure to keep the molding in a straight line. If you are using the first type of molding, you can help hold it in place with clamps or holders. The metal clamps for brooms are good for this purpose. They look like this:

They can be purchased at most hardware stores.

Just screw them onto a piece of wood as shown and insert a piece of molding.

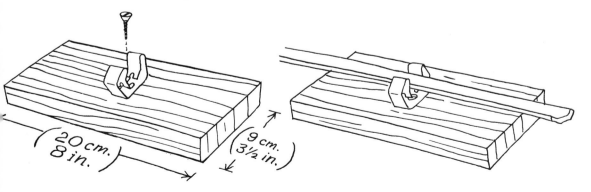

20 cm.
8 in.

9 cm.
3½ in.

Since type *B* molding is wider, you can simply tape it in place with masking tape.

CONNECTING MOLDINGS

If you want the balls to travel more than eight feet, you will have to join two or more pieces of molding together. A simple way of doing this is described here.

You will need:

      pieces of wood, about 6 cm. (2½ in.) wide and 24 cm.
        (10 in.) long
      12 nails with small heads

Step 1. Place a piece of molding on top of the wood.
Step 2. Hammer six nails on each side, evenly spaced. Bang the nails into the wood until the heads touch the molding.

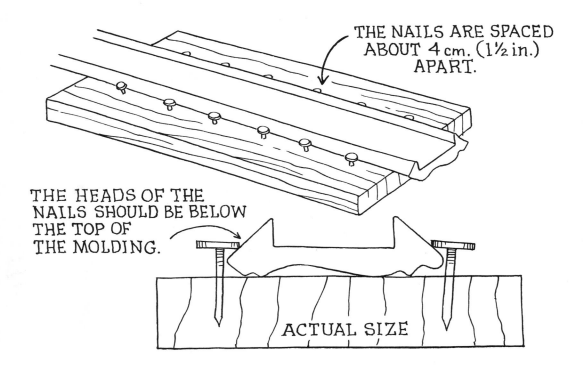

THE NAILS ARE SPACED ABOUT 4 cm. (1½ in.) APART.

THE HEADS OF THE NAILS SHOULD BE BELOW THE TOP OF THE MOLDING.

ACTUAL SIZE

Step 3. Move the pieces of molding back so only three sets of nails are holding it. Then slide the second piece of molding between the other set of nails. Push the ends of the two pieces together.

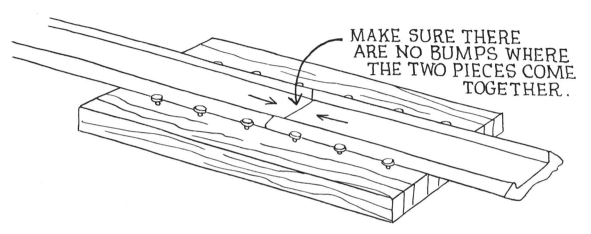

MAKE SURE THERE ARE NO BUMPS WHERE THE TWO PIECES COME TOGETHER.

When joining the molding together, make sure they are lined up straight. Tape the wood holding the connectors and holders down to the floor, table, or chair you have laid the track on. This will keep it from moving around as the balls roll down it.

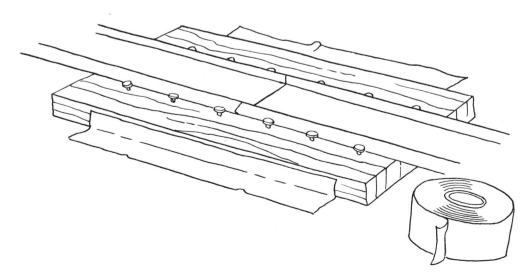

A BALL-RELEASE MECHANISM

In some of the games and experiments shown in this book, it is helpful to have a device that releases balls automatically. With a few changes, an ordinary electric doorbell can do this.

You will need:

> 2-pole electric doorbell with clapper and switch
>
> 2 pieces of wood, one piece approximately $2\frac{1}{2}$ cm. $\times$ 20 cm. (1 in. $\times$ 8 in.), the other 20 cm. $\times$ $22\frac{1}{2}$ cm. (8 in. $\times$ 9 in.)
>
> nails
>
> tongue depressor or Popsicle stick
>
> C-clamp
>
> 2 D-cell batteries
>
> battery holder (optional)
>
> electrical wire
>
> masking tape

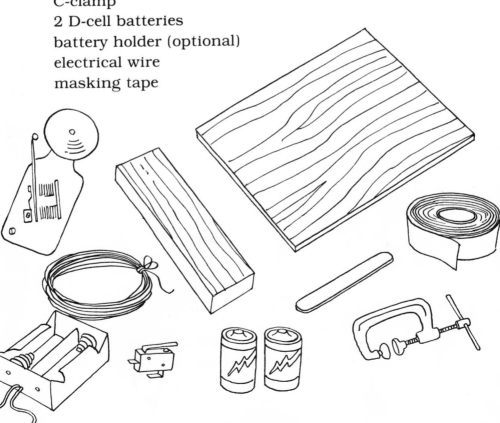

When you attach wires to certain points on an electrical doorbell, the clapper can do one of two things. If you attach wires to points *A* and *B*, the clapper moves back and forth without stopping until you turn off the electricity.

If you attach wires to points *B* and *C*, the clapper stays against the bell until you turn off the electricity.

By sending electricity to points *B* and *C*, the clapper will release one ball at a time onto the track.

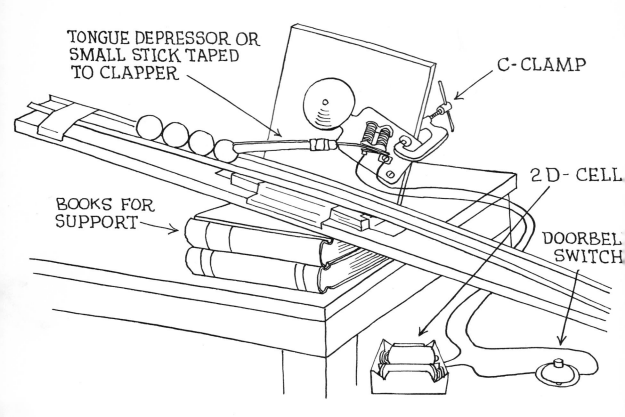

TONGUE DEPRESSOR OR
SMALL STICK TAPED
TO CLAPPER

C-CLAMP

2 D-CELL

BOOKS FOR
SUPPORT

DOORBELL
SWITCH

Here's how to assemble the ball-release mechanism:

Step 1. Nail the two pieces of wood together to form a right angle. They will support the track and doorbell.

Step 2. Tape a small piece of wood, such as a Popsicle stick, to the clapper of the bell.

Step 3. Tape the track in place on the wood support.

Step 4. Clamp the doorbell loosely on the wood support as shown in the drawing above. Connect the electrical wires to the bell and to the battery holder.

Step 5. Adjust the position of the bell so that the Popsicle stick will keep the balls from rolling but will let them move when the electricity is turned on. You will have to experiment to find out how long to leave the electricity on, so that only one ball at a time rolls down.

If you want to space the release of balls more precisely, you can use the doorbell to let the balls go automatically, too.

You will need:

      record player
      micro switch (this can be purchased from electronic
           supply stores)
      piece of cardboard, about 5 cm. (2 in.) long
      masking tape

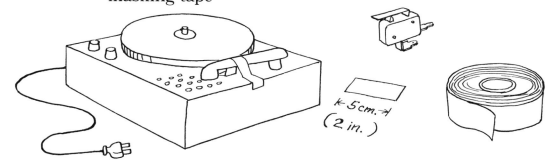

A micro switch works just like other switches, except that it takes very little pressure to turn it on and off.

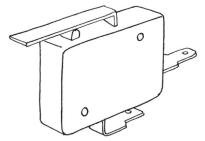

The most widely available micro switches usually have three contact points. If you hook up two of these to the batteries, the switch lets the electricity flow only when you depress it. However, if you hook up two of the three contact points another way, electricity is always flowing and is only turned off when you depress the switch. You will have to experiment to determine which contact points to use for your particular switch.

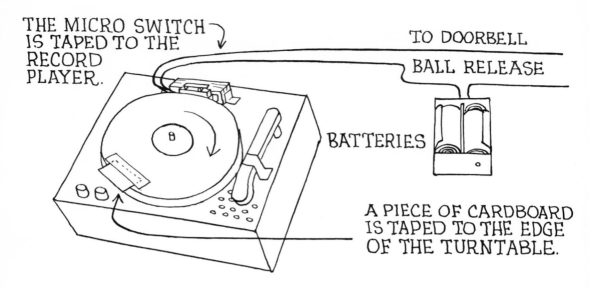

THE MICRO SWITCH IS TAPED TO THE RECORD PLAYER.

TO DOORBELL

BALL RELEASE

BATTERIES

A PIECE OF CARDBOARD IS TAPED TO THE EDGE OF THE TURNTABLE.

As the turntable revolves, the piece of cardboard hits the lever of the micro switch, turning on the electricity. The longer the piece of cardboard, the longer the electricity is turned on. When the turntable speed is set at $33\frac{1}{3}$, a 2-inch piece of cardboard should cause the clapper to stay up long enough to let one ball go.

BEFORE YOU START

All the track arrangements described here do work. They have been tried out many times. If you find the ball doesn't stay on the track the first time you roll it down, check carefully to see that the molding is in a straight line, that the places where two pieces of molding are connected are smooth, and that the molding is not bent in any way.

Any kind of ball can be used in these games, as long as it stays on the track. Marbles are all right and are usually uniform in size and weight, which is necessary for some of the experiments.

Straight Tracks

Some of the easiest types of games you can play with your
tracks are races. You can have balls race against each other
or against the clock. Even though you won't be able to get
exact times, you can make close estimates of how long it took
for the balls to roll down. Not only will you have fun playing
the games in this section, but also they'll help you understand along the way the different kinds of motions of objects.

RACING BALLS

The simplest type of track you can make is the one described here. Attach the molding to a board, then rest one end of the board on a table and the other end on the floor. If you line up another piece of molding alongside the first, you can have races.

A STICK HOLDS BACK THE BALLS.

A WOODEN BOARD SUPPORTS THE TRACKS.

To hold back the balls at the top, use a stick that goes across both tracks. Then, when you release the balls, both of them will start at the same time. Put a piece of wood at the bottom. By listening for the sounds of the balls hitting the board, you'll be able to tell which ball arrived at the end first. If you can't tell the two hits apart, that means there's a tie.

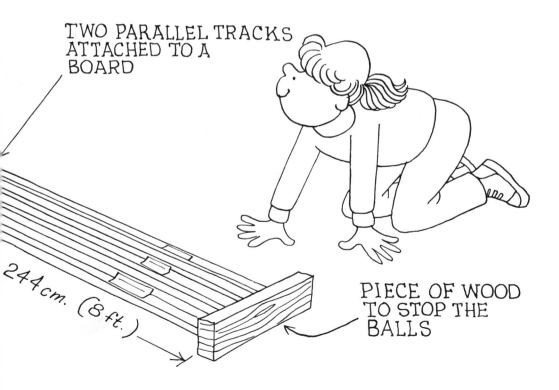

TWO PARALLEL TRACKS ATTACHED TO A BOARD

244 cm. (8 ft.)

PIECE OF WOOD TO STOP THE BALLS

Games and Experiments to Try

- Get some wooden and plastic beads from a crafts store. Also, look in the telephone book's *Yellow Pages* under "Bearings" to see where steel ball bearings are sold, and get several different sizes. Race each of these balls against a marble. Do any of them move faster than a marble down the track?
- Make the tracks longer. Does the length of the track make any difference in which type of ball wins?
- Raise one track higher than the other. Does the angle of the track make any difference in the speed of the ball? Does a higher starting point make the ball go faster?

What's Happening?

If you have done these races carefully, you should find that even though the balls are different sizes and weights, all roll down the track and reach the bottom at the same time. And, as you raise the slant of the track, the balls move faster.

Based on careful experimentation and thinking, scientists such as Isaac Newton and Galileo arrived at the conclusion that all objects fall at the same speed vertically, regardless of their weight and size. If you were to release a feather and a steel ball together in a tube that has no air, they would reach the bottom at the same time. (In the real world, however, air resistance slows down the falling feather.) Similarly, balls of different weights rolling on the same kind of track will have the same speeds.

Slanting the track more steeply makes the ball roll faster. The rate at which the ball's speed increases is called *acceleration*. To understand how this happens, you need to picture two forces. The earth pulls on the ball with a certain amount of force that is always the same no matter how slanted the track is. This force is called *gravity*. The track is exerting a force on the ball opposite to the pull of the earth. These two forces are equal and opposite when the track is horizontal. Therefore, the ball doesn't move.

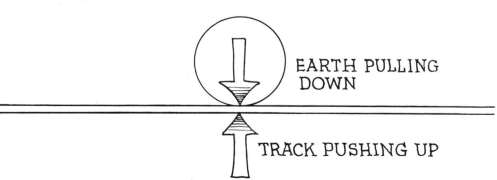

EARTH PULLING DOWN

TRACK PUSHING UP

When you slant the track, the ball is still pulled to the earth with the same force, but the track is no longer pushing back with an equal force. This results in the ball rolling to the earth.

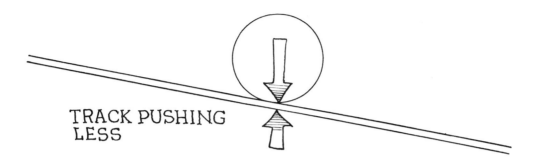

TRACK PUSHING LESS

The more you slant the track, the less the track supports the ball. The greater the force on the ball, the faster it moves.

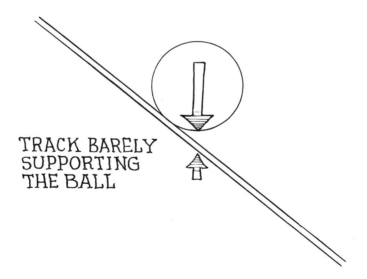

TRACK BARELY SUPPORTING THE BALL

You will get a better idea of what acceleration means when you play the other games in this section.

MOVING TARGET

In the previous game you found that slanting the track more steeply makes the ball accelerate, or roll much faster. Just how much faster does the ball travel when the angle of the track is changed? Is the difference a matter of seconds or fractions of a second?

Here is a game you can play that will challenge your skill in timing and give you an approximation of the acceleration of the ball. The object of this game is to roll a ball down the track into the cup while the record turntable is moving.

BOOKS OR TAPE HOLD DOWN THE TRACK.

TAPE SIDES OF TRACK TO A CHAIR.

POINT A

Before turning the record player on, roll a ball down the track and see if it falls into the cup when the cup is at point A. If it doesn't, adjust the position of the record player until the ball does.

Once you turn the record player on and the cup starts revolving, your timing will have to be very careful. You will have to watch the revolving cup and find some point in its rotation where you should always release the ball.

To make it easy in the beginning, start at the slowest speed, $33\frac{1}{3}$ rpm.

What's Happening?

When the turntable is moving at $33\frac{1}{3}$ rpm, it makes one full revolution about every 2 seconds.

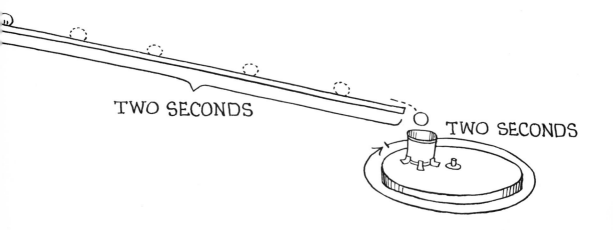

TWO SECONDS

TWO SECONDS

This means that if the ball is released when the cup is at point *A* and the ball falls into the cup when it returns to point *A*, the ball has taken 2 seconds to travel down the track.

- By raising or lowering the track, can you find the angle, or height, at which the ball travels down the track and goes into the cup after the cup has made one full revolution?

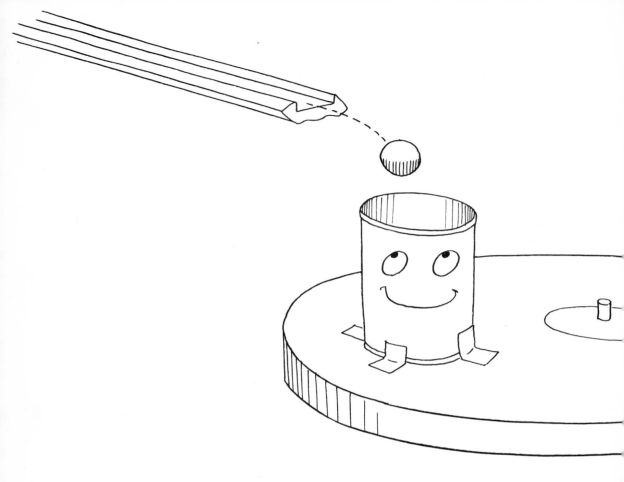

Further Challenges

- Can you get the ball into the cup when the turntable is moving at 45 or 78 rpm?
- Can you get the ball into the cup when the track is two or three times longer?
- Cut a circle from cardboard that is larger in diameter than the turntable. Tape this to the turntable, place the cup on the cardboard, and see if you can get the ball into the cup now. (Remember that even though the cardboard circle is larger, the cup is still making one revolution in the same amount of time as when it is just on the turntable.)

A Greater Challenge

In this game the balls are released automatically, using the doorbell and micro switch. Set up the track and automatic ball-release mechanism like this:

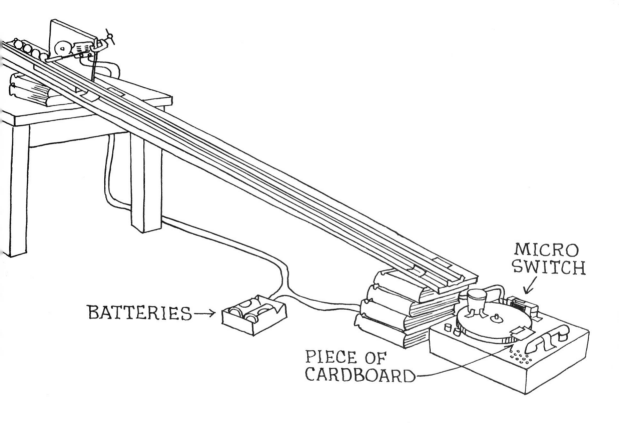

BATTERIES→

MICRO SWITCH

PIECE OF CARDBOARD→

Tape a 5-cm. (2-in.) piece of cardboard to the edge of the turntable. When the cardboard goes past the micro switch, a ball should be released. If you position the micro switch at the right spot on the record player, each ball should roll into the cup. Start with the $33\frac{1}{3}$ speed, then go to a higher speed. (Remember that when you change the speed, you will have to change the position of the micro switch.)

THE ZIGZAG GAME

Here is a ball and track game that has been popular for a long time. The kind that you see in department stores is usually small. You can make a larger and more exciting one for yourself using the plastic molding. The track looks like this when it is assembled:

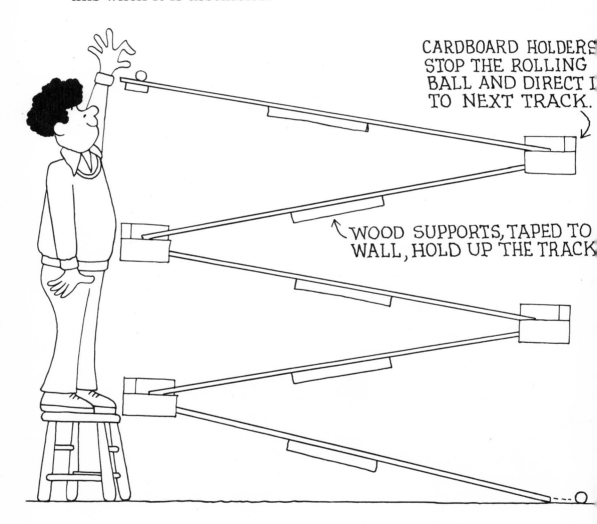

CARDBOARD HOLDERS
STOP THE ROLLING
BALL AND DIRECT I
TO NEXT TRACK.

WOOD SUPPORTS, TAPED TO
WALL, HOLD UP THE TRACK

To assemble the cardboard holders:

Step 1. Cut the cardboard and fold it as shown here.

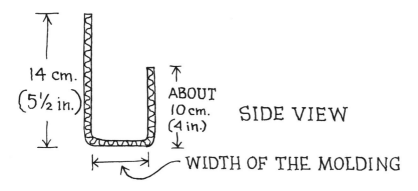

14 cm.
(5½ in.)

ABOUT
10 cm.
(4 in.)

SIDE VIEW

WIDTH OF THE MOLDING

Step 2. Cut two pieces of wood and tape one to the back of the cardboard holder and the other to the track.

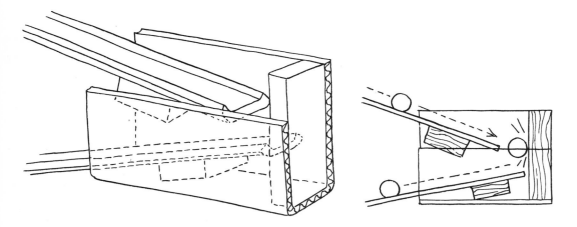

Tape the pieces of molding to a wall or a large piece of cardboard. Try to line up the tracks so that all are at the same angle. Then tape the cardboard holders at each end of the track, making sure the ball has room to roll through the holder to the track below.

Games and Experiments to Try

- How long does it take for a ball to travel down five tracks all at the same angle?
- Make the angles of the track steeper. How will this change the total time of travel?
- Try several angles. What is the slowest you can make the balls travel and still get to the bottom?

What's Happening?

If you find the total time it takes for a ball to travel down all five tracks, you can divide by five and get the time it takes to travel on one track. This assumes that all of the tracks are at the same angle. It also assumes that the ball doesn't stop when it hits the cardboard holder at the end of the track.

How does this time compare with the time you got in the Moving Target Game?

Further Challenges

- Can you arrange the angle or the length of the tracks so that a ball takes very close to five seconds to run down all five of them?
- Using the doorbell ball-release mechanism and the micro switch, you can make a ball turn on the switch when it reaches the bottom of the tracks and release another ball at the top.

    This arrangement is not so much an experiment as a challenge in engineering. The doorbell ball-release mechanism has been shown back on page 12. The track is set up the same as for the Zigzag Game.

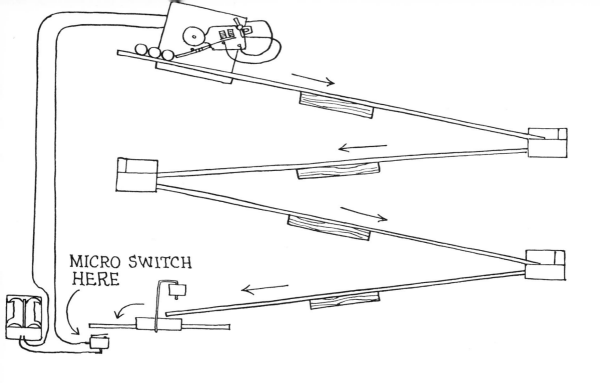

MICRO SWITCH
HERE

This is how the micro switch setup is assembled:

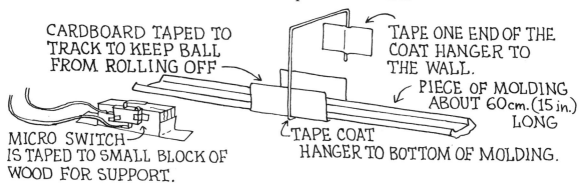

CARDBOARD TAPED TO
TRACK TO KEEP BALL
FROM ROLLING OFF

TAPE ONE END OF THE
COAT HANGER TO
THE WALL.

PIECE OF MOLDING
ABOUT 60cm. (15 in.)
LONG

MICRO SWITCH
IS TAPED TO SMALL BLOCK OF
WOOD FOR SUPPORT.

TAPE COAT
HANGER TO BOTTOM OF MOLDING.

The track is balanced like a seesaw using a sturdy wire or
a piece of a coat hanger taped to the bottom of the molding
as the fulcrum. Position the device so that when the ball
falls onto this track, it will roll forward, causing the track
to hit the micro switch.

MUSICAL TRACKS

You can make the tracks from the Zigzag Game into a music machine by hanging small bells or pieces of metal above the track. When the ball rolls down, it hits these and produces interesting pitches and rhythms. The musical tracks are set up like this:

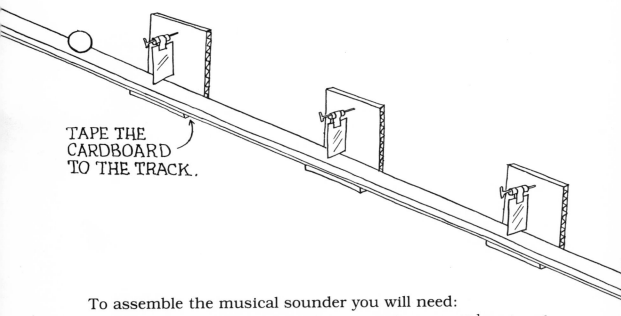

TAPE THE
CARDBOARD
TO THE TRACK.

To assemble the musical sounder you will need:

> 8 to 10 pieces of cardboard, each 6 cm. ($2\frac{1}{2}$ in.) wide and 10 cm. (4 in.) long
>
> T-pins
>
> pieces of tubing, such as plastic drinking straws, each cut about $1\frac{1}{2}$ cm. ($\frac{1}{2}$ in.) long
>
> pieces of metal, each 4 cm. ($1\frac{1}{2}$ in.) long (You can use either pieces of metal strapping used for crates; or thin metal washers, called fender washers; or small bells.)
>
> masking tape

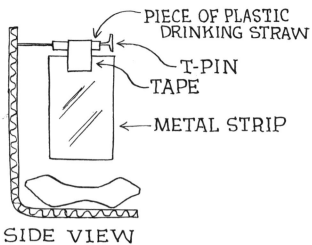

PIECE OF PLASTIC
DRINKING STRAW

T-PIN

TAPE

METAL STRIP

SIDE VIEW

Step 1. Bend the cardboard so that it fits under the track and tape it to the bottom of the track.

Step 2. Tape the metal strip, washer, or bell to the drinking-straw tube.

Step 3. Insert the T-pin through the tube and push it securely into the cardboard.

The gap between the metal strip and the track should be wide enough so that half the ball will be below the bottom edge of the metal.

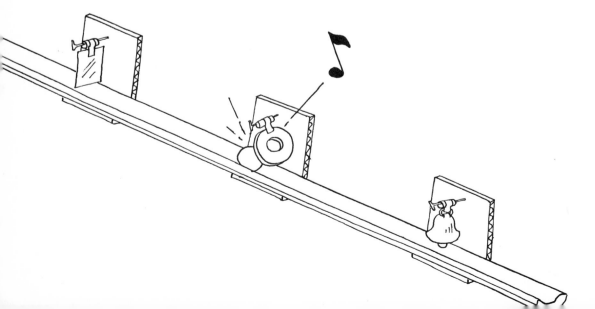

Games and Experiments to Try

Place a musical sounder every 15 cm. (6 in.) from top to bottom.

Let the ball roll down the track several times and listen very carefully.

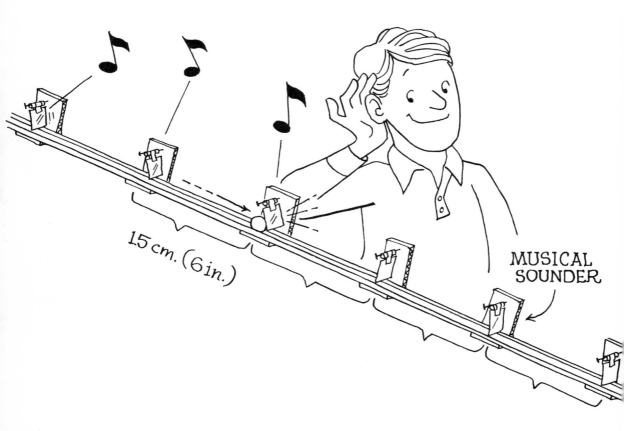

- Are all the sounds equally spaced?
- How do the sounds change if you slant the track more steeply?
- Will the timing of the sounds be different if you use balls of different sizes and weights?

Next, set up a track that is partly slanted and partly horizontal. You will need at least two pieces of molding connected together.

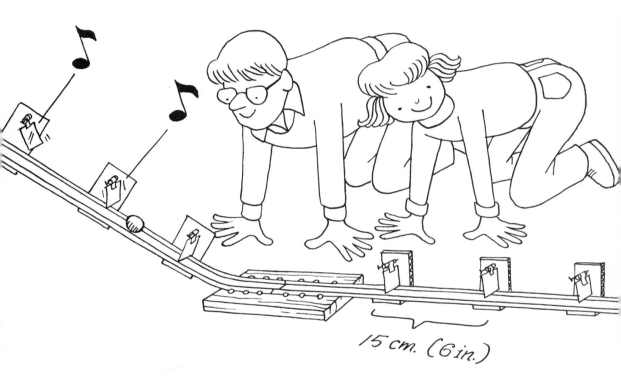

15 cm. (6 in.)

- Are the sounds equally spaced when the ball rolls on the horizontal part of the track?

What's Happening?

On the slanted track, the sounds of the ball hitting the metal strips are not equally spaced. The farther down the slant, the closer together the sounds are. This tells you that the ball is traveling faster at the bottom of the track than at the top of it. That is, during equal amounts of time, the ball travels greater distances. This type of motion is called *acceleration.*

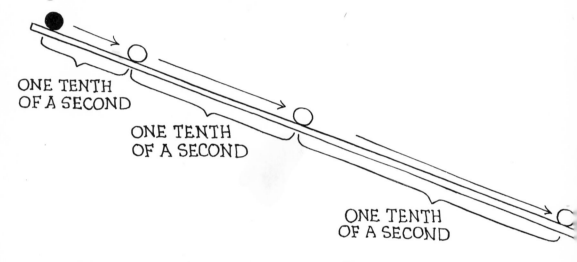

ONE TENTH OF A SECOND

ONE TENTH OF A SECOND

ONE TENTH OF A SECOND

However, when the ball traveling down the slanted track comes to the horizontal part, the sounds are equally spaced. This is because the ball is no longer accelerating. It travels equal distances during equal amounts of time. This type of motion, with unchanging speed, is called *velocity.*

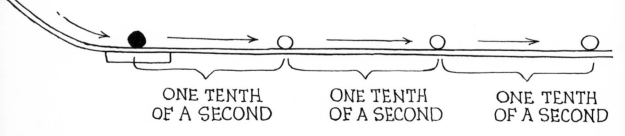

ONE TENTH OF A SECOND

ONE TENTH OF A SECOND

ONE TENTH OF A SECOND

If this horizontal part of the track were very, very long, you would see the ball slowing down. The rubbing of the ball against the track, or *friction*, causes this. However, for the first part of the track, the ball tends to travel at the same speed.

You will see the effects of friction better in the next set of games.

Circles and Curves

In all the games so far, the balls traveled straight down a slanted track. What happens when the track is curved?

THE BIG U

The simplest type of curved track is the U-shape. With this arrangement you can make all kinds of games.

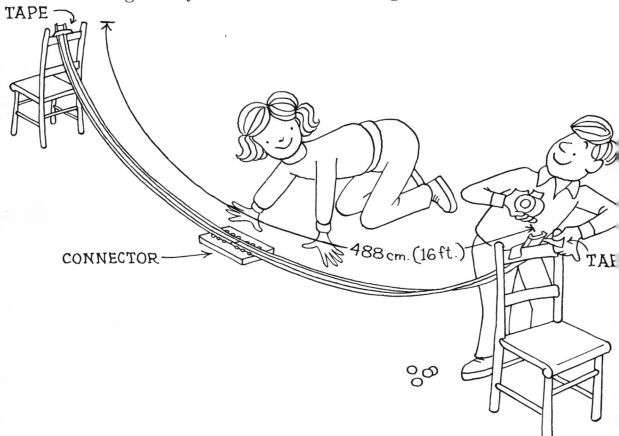

TAPE

CONNECTOR

488 cm. (16 ft.)

TAPE

Games and Experiments to Try

- Can you get the ball to the other end of the track without pushing it?
- Can you get two balls moving back and forth on the track without them hitting each other?

What happens when you change the shape of the U in the following ways?

- Move the two chairs farther apart or tape the molding lower down the back of the chairs.

- Lower only one side of the track.

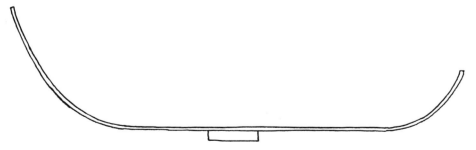

- Position the track so that the middle portion runs along the floor.

Further Challenges

Set up the following arrangement:

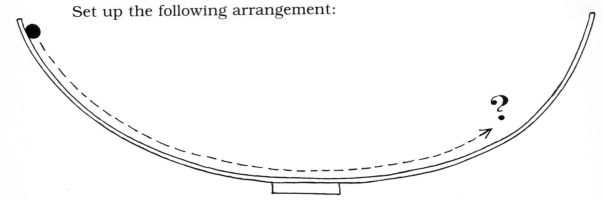

- Release a ball at the very top of the track. How far will it travel up on the other side? Make a mark on the track.
- Try balls of different weights and sizes. Record how far up each ball travels on the other side.
- How many times will each ball travel back and forth before it comes to a complete stop?
- Is there a difference between heavy and light balls?
- Now change the shape of the track to look like this:

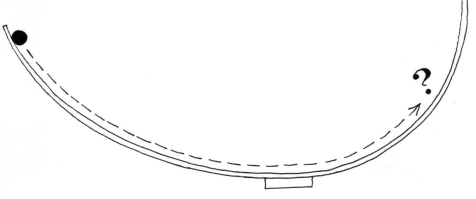

Does the shape of the track make any difference in how far up the various balls travel?

What's Happening?

In the "ideal" world, a ball released on one side of the Big U track would travel to the same height on the other side. However, in the real world, as the ball rolls down the track, it is both sliding and rolling. (If you roll a heavy metal ball, you can sometimes actually see this sliding.) This sliding, or friction, lessens the amount of energy the ball has as it goes down the track and also as it rises up on the other side. Not having the amount of energy it started with, the ball doesn't make it to the top. Each time it rolls back and forth, it loses more and more energy, and eventually it stops.

Some balls go higher as they roll down and up the track the first time, and will continue to roll longer than others. This is because each ball acquires a certain amount of energy as it rolls down the track, depending on its speed and weight. As you saw in the previous games and experiments, balls of different weights have the same speed at the bottom of the track. But a heavier ball traveling at the same speed as a lighter one has more energy. So, although both balls are being slowed by friction, the larger amount of energy of the heavier one keeps it going longer.

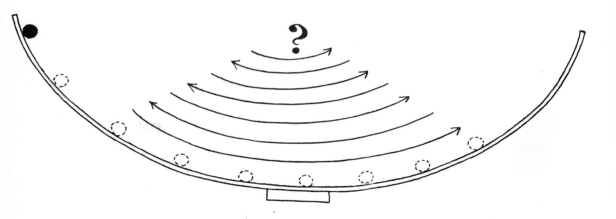

ROLLER COASTER

Balls roll back and forth on the Big U. How will they travel on a series of Big Us connected together? Of course, this is another way of describing a roller coaster in an amusement park. Here is one way you could assemble it:

Remember to keep the track in a straight line. The molding should not have any twists or bends in it. All connections should be smooth.

Depending on how many pieces of molding you have and how big the room is, your roller coaster can be as long as you want to make it.

Games and Experiments to Try

- Using just two pieces of molding, what is the most number of hills and valleys you can make and still keep the ball rolling on the track?
- Can you arrange the molding so that the ball will just about make it over each hill?
- Will a ball make it to the end if it is released on the second or third hill?
- Does a heavier ball roll differently than a lighter one?

What's Happening?

As you found out by experimenting with the Big U, the ball gains energy by traveling down the slanted track. The higher the ball's starting point, the greater the energy it has at the bottom. On top of each hill the amount of energy the ball has is called *potential energy.*

When you place a ball in the valley, or bottom, of the Big U, it doesn't go anywhere. Its potential energy is zero. However, when it rolls into this valley from the top of the track, it keeps on traveling. The ball at that point is said to have *kinetic energy.* The kinetic energy of the moving ball enables it to travel up the next hill.

On the Roller Coaster track the ball is continually changing its potential energy into kinetic energy. As it rolls down, it gains more and more kinetic energy and has the most at the bottom of the valley. It gains more and more potential energy as it rolls to the top of the next hill. However, as the ball travels up and down the hills of the Roller Coaster, it keeps losing energy because of friction. That is why you have to arrange your track so that each succeeding hill is lower than the last one.

Many systems in nature are similar to this changing back and forth of potential and kinetic energy. Pendulums such as a swing in a playground, bouncing springs such as a Slinky, and water waves in a bathtub will each keep moving back and forth until they eventually run out of energy.

LOOP THE LOOP

On some roller coasters, especially the really giant ones, there is a section called the Loop the Loop. Here the cars travel around in a big circle, and at one point the people inside them are upside down. You can create the same arrangement with the molding.

To make this track you will need *flexible* plastic molding. Be careful when bending it into a circle because some plastic is not too flexible and may break.

Start out with a small loop about 56 cm. (22 in.) in diameter. The ball has to start rolling from a certain height if it is going to make it around the loop. You will have to experiment to find that starting point.

Games and Experiments to Try

- What is the biggest loop you can make and still have the ball travel around it without stopping or falling off?
- Can you make the ball travel through two or three loops in a row?
- Can you get the ball to fly into a can placed near the end of the track?

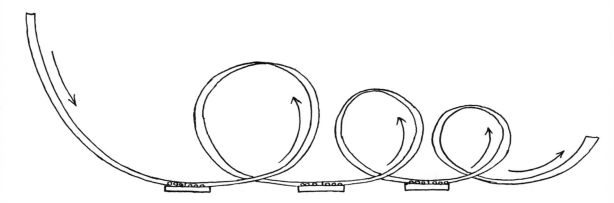

- Make a combination of a Loop the Loop and a Big U.

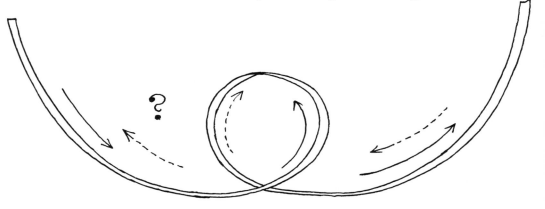

- What happens to the ball on this track?

What's Happening?

If you could take pictures of what was happening to the ball on the Loop the Loop, here is what you might see.

If the ball started rolling from the highest part of the track:

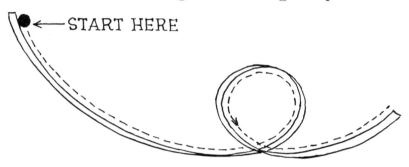

If the ball started rolling from the middle of the slanted track:

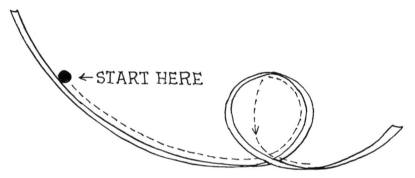

If the ball started rolling from near the bottom of the slanted part of the track:

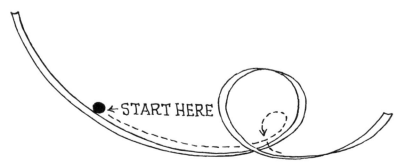

As you saw with the Big U, the ball is fighting friction as it rolls down the track. With the Loop the Loop, it also has to fight the downward pull of gravity as it rises to the top of the loop. The higher up you start the ball rolling, the more likely it is to make it around the loop. The greater the speed of the ball, the more force is needed to change the direction in which it is moving. When the ball has sufficient speed, it wants to keep moving in the direction of the track instead of being pulled downward by gravity. Therefore, it is more likely to make it around the Loop the Loop than to fall off.

In this kind of situation the ball is said to have *momentum*. The greater the momentum, the greater is the force needed to stop the ball or to change its direction.

When you widen the size of the loop, the ball must have greater momentum to make it around this larger loop. So, the track before the loop must be longer or steeper.

CIRCULAR RACEWAY

The Loop the Loop is a game in which the ball travels around
a vertical circle. It can also travel around a horizontal one.
You can make this type of arrangement easily by just
bending the molding at the bottom of a slanted track into a
circle and laying it on the floor.

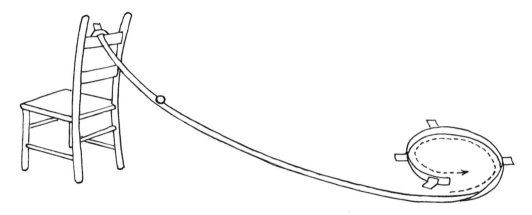

A more interesting arrangement is shown in the next
drawing. Here the ball travels in a circle somewhat vertically
and somewhat horizontally as it rolls around the inside of a
cone.

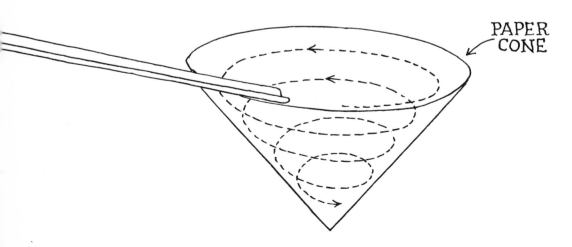

PAPER
CONE

To construct the cone you will need:

  piece of very heavy paper that will hold its shape
    when folded (You can find this paper at a
    stationery store. The larger the paper, the more
    exciting the game.) Linoleum carpet can also be
    used.
  piece of cardboard, at least half the length of the
    paper
  pencil
  thumbtack or nail
  scissors
  masking tape

Step 1. Using the piece of cardboard as a compass, draw a
circle as wide as the paper.

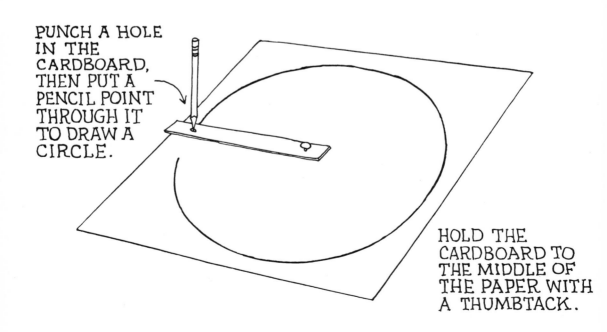

PUNCH A HOLE
IN THE
CARDBOARD,
THEN PUT A
PENCIL POINT
THROUGH IT
TO DRAW A
CIRCLE.

HOLD THE
CARDBOARD TO
THE MIDDLE OF
THE PAPER WITH
A THUMBTACK.

Step 2. Cut out the circle. Then cut a straight line that goes from the edge of the circle to the center.

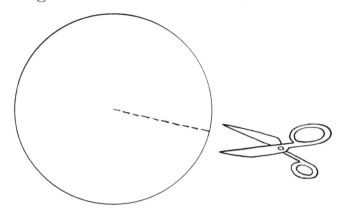

Step 3. Fold the paper circle into a cone shape and tape both edges *lightly.* (You should tape lightly so that you can change the shape later.)

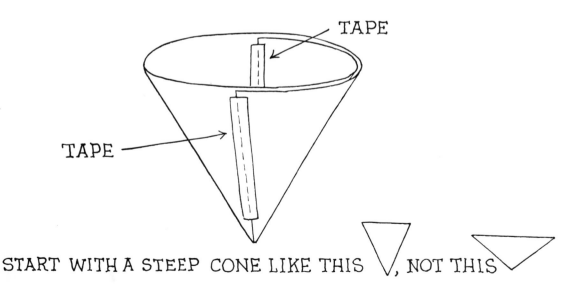

START WITH A STEEP CONE LIKE THIS ∨, NOT THIS ▽

Step 4. Rest the cone inside a bucket or wastepaper basket.

The challenge in this game is to roll the ball onto the edge of the cone and have it travel around in a circle. You may have to adjust the height of the track and the angle at which the ball enters the cone. When the arrangement is working right, the ball should travel around the cone several times before it stops at the bottom.

Games and Experiments to Try

- What is the most number of times you can get the ball to circle inside the cone?
- Does the weight or size of the ball make a difference in the number of times it travels around the cone?
- What happens when you change the shape of the cone to look like each of these?

- On which cone shape will it circle the longest?
- Can you get four or five balls traveling on the cone at the same time?

What's Happening?

When the ball rolls off the track, it wants to move in a straight line, but the sides of the cone direct it into a circle. The ball is traveling with a momentum that helps it fight the downward pull of gravity.

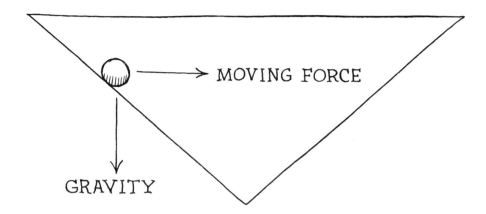

MOVING FORCE

GRAVITY

This momentum is related to the speed of the ball. As friction slows it down, the ball feels the pull of gravity more and more. So, it gradually falls toward the center of the cone.

If you were to eliminate friction and gravity, the ball would continue to move in a circle at the same height continuously. You can get some idea of this by doing the next challenge.

further Challenge

- Take the cone out of the bucket and hold it. Place a ball inside the cone. Can you get the ball to travel on the side of the cone in a circle, keeping it at exactly the same height? (If you use a large bowl instead of the cone, this is easier to do.) The force you need to keep the ball circling is not great, but the timing is important.

Flying and Colliding Balls

In all the previous games, the ball's direction and speed were determined by the shape of the track. However, when the ball leaves the track, it has a certain amount of speed and momentum. What pathway does the ball take as it falls to the ground? What momentum does a ball have as it leaves the track?

The next set of games will help you answer these questions.

JUMP THE GAP

Stunt-car drivers and motorcyclists like to come up a ramp at great speed, fly off the ramp, and land on another one. Before they can do this, though, they have to do some careful planning. You can get a sense of how they plan this by setting up a similar situation with two tracks and a rolling ball.

Rest a track between a chair and a stool, placing tape as shown in the drawing so that the track won't move. You will have to experiment to find exactly how far away the second track should be placed. Start out with a gap of only a few inches.

In setting up the games in this section, the arrangement of the moldings has to be very precise. They will work better if you tape a piece of cardboard on the second track to prevent the ball from jumping off when it lands.

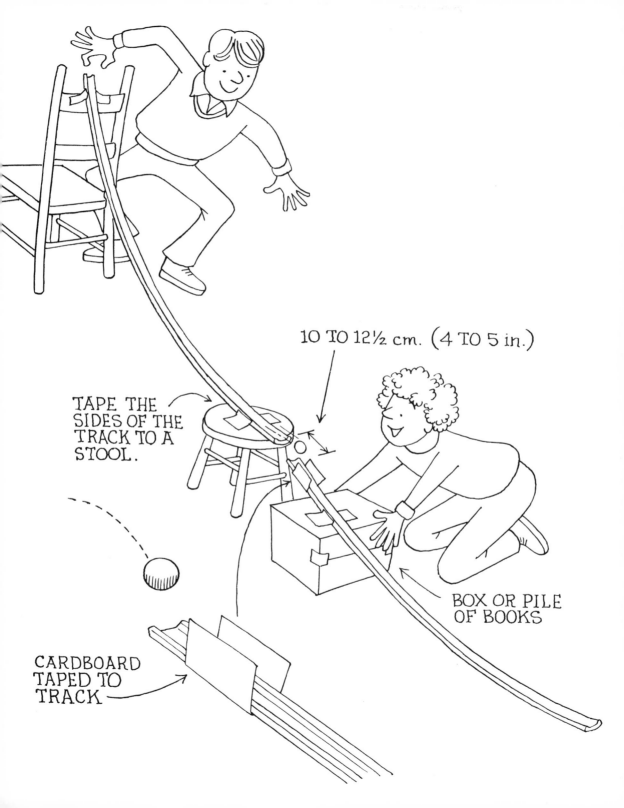

10 TO 12½ cm. (4 TO 5 in.)

TAPE THE
SIDES OF THE
TRACK TO A
STOOL.

BOX OR PILE
OF BOOKS

CARDBOARD
TAPED TO
TRACK

Games and Experiments to Try

- How far apart can you make the gap in each arrangement and still have the ball land on the other track?
- Do heavier balls jump the gap better than lighter ones?
- Does it make any difference if the first half of the track is made longer?
- Here are some other arrangements you can try:

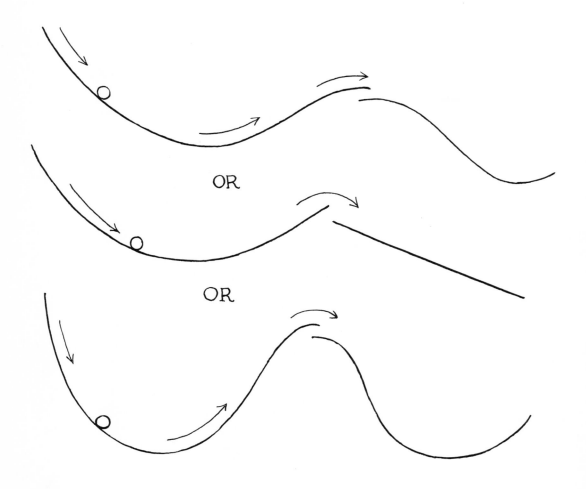

OR

OR

What's Happening?

As soon as the ball leaves the first track, the downward pull of gravity acts on it, causing it to fall toward the floor. As in the other games, the greater the speed of the ball upon leaving the track, the more momentum it has, so it can fight gravity longer and travel farther before falling. Therefore, the longer the first track and the steeper the slant, the farther the ball will travel when it leaves the track.

By doing the next experiment, you will be able to plot the pathway the ball takes when it leaves the track.

Further Challenge

- To see what happens to the ball when it leaves the track, set up an arrangement that looks like this:

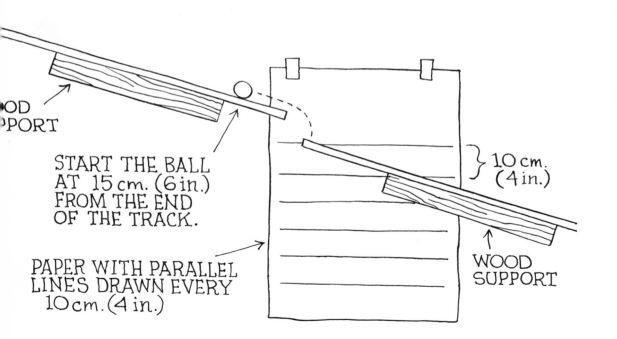

OD
PORT

START THE BALL
AT 15 cm. (6 in.)
FROM THE END
OF THE TRACK.

PAPER WITH PARALLEL
LINES DRAWN EVERY
10 cm. (4 in.)

$\}$ 10 cm.
(4 in.)

WOOD
SUPPORT

Tape two pieces of molding or a large piece of cardboard to a wall as shown in the previous drawing. Get a large piece of paper and draw a series of lines on it every 10 cm. (4 in.). Tape the paper behind the second track. Roll the ball down the first track and try to get it to land on the very tip of the second track. Do this several times to make sure the second track is positioned at the best spot. Mark on the paper where the second track ends.

Move the second track 10 cm. (4 in.) lower and find where the best spot is to just catch the ball. Do this for four of five different levels.

If you are careful in doing this, you should get a curve that bends something like this:

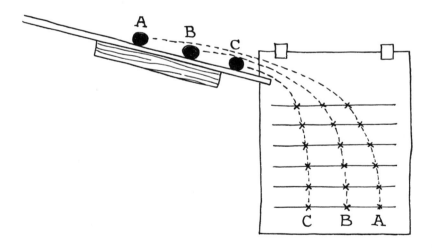

You will find that the farther up you start the ball, the farther the ball will travel. But all of the pathways will be curved.

SKI JUMP

On television you have probably seen skiers slide down a big long slope, hit a ramp and fly into the air, then land far away from the ramp. You can create the same kind of arrangement with molding and a ball and make a game of it.

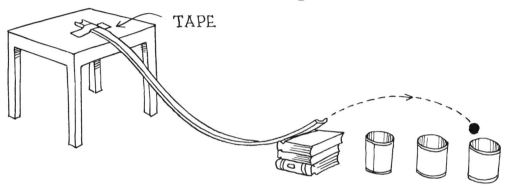

TAPE

Games and Experiments to Try

- Can you get the ball to fly into each of the buckets?
- Does the size or weight of the ball make any difference in how the ball will fly off the end of the track?
- If you make the slanted part longer, will the ball fly farther away from the track?
- What happens if you keep the slanted part of the track the same but make the curved part steeper or flatter?

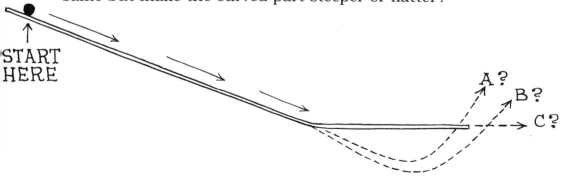

START HERE

A?
B?
C?

- Does the ball travel different distances for each curve?

What's Happening?

If you watch carefully, you should find that the middle curve, B, lets the ball travel the farthest:

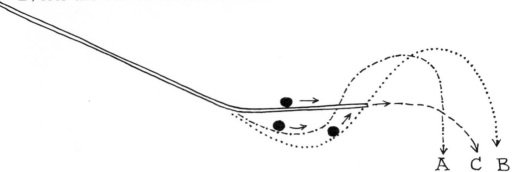

The best angle is halfway between the vertical and the horizontal:

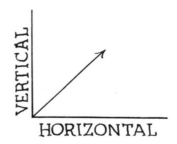

Further Challenges

When the ball leaves the track, it is not easy to see the pathway it takes. Here is an arrangement that will not only test your skill but also will help you follow the ball's direction better. The object of this game is to roll the ball down the track and get it into the box.

You will need a large, flat piece of cardboard or a piece of plywood and a small box or paper cup cut in half lengthwise.

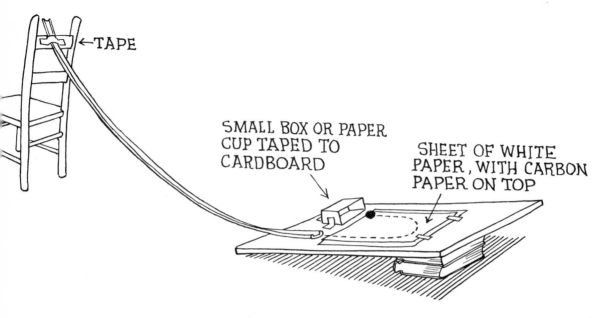

←TAPE

SMALL BOX OR PAPER
CUP TAPED TO
CARDBOARD

SHEET OF WHITE
PAPER, WITH CARBON
PAPER ON TOP

- Try to get the ball to roll slowly and watch carefully how it travels. (If you use a heavy metal ball, you can trace its pathway by putting a piece of white paper down on the cardboard and then a piece of carbon paper on top.)
- Try moving the track different distances from the box as well as at several different angles and see what happens.

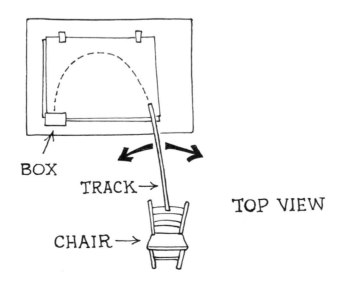

BOX

TRACK→

CHAIR→

TOP VIEW

BILLIARDS

Billiards and pool are popular games where balls are sent crashing into each other. Some players are very skillful and can knock the balls into the holes, or pockets, very easily. It takes careful planning to do this. You can get some idea of how it is done by setting up the following arrangement:

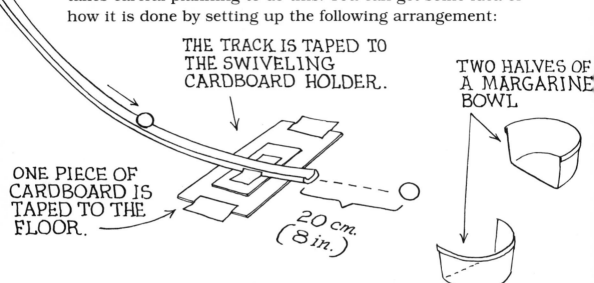

THE TRACK IS TAPED TO THE SWIVELING CARDBOARD HOLDER..

TWO HALVES OF A MARGARINE BOWL

ONE PIECE OF CARDBOARD IS TAPED TO THE FLOOR.

20 cm. (8 in.)

The holder for the track is made out of two pieces of cardboard that are held together in the middle with a brass fastener.

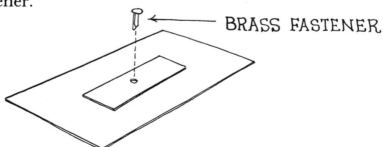

BRASS FASTENER

This setup allows you to move the track to different angles easily.

Make a mark on the floor about 20 cm. (8 in.) from the end of the track and carefully rest the ball there. (This game works best with large balls, so try to get large marbles or golf balls.) Use a plastic margarine cup cut in half lengthwise for the pocket.

Games and Experiments to Try

- Can you roll a ball down the track and have it hit the other ball into one of the cups?
- Can you get the ball into the same cup ten times in a row?
- Can you roll the ball down the track so that one goes into one cup and the other goes into the other cup?
- Now try moving the cups farther apart and at different angles to the ball on the floor. See how far apart you can place the cups and still hit the balls into them.

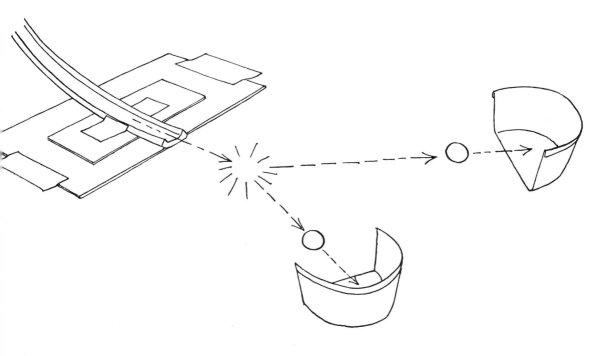

What's Happening?

If you tried different experiments with the billiard arrangement, you may have noticed a pattern to the way in which the balls rolled after collision. To understand what is happening, first picture that there is a line drawn through the center of the ball at rest on the floor.

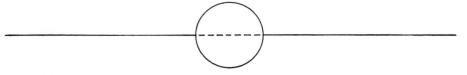

When the rolling ball hits the resting ball head-on, the two should continue traveling in the same direction.

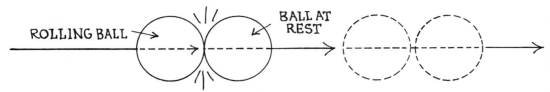

When the rolling ball hits the resting ball off-center, each ball can roll in many directions.

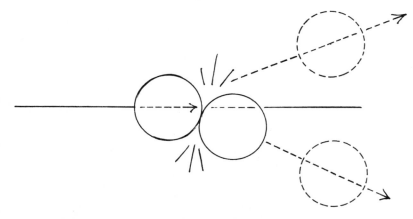

The farther off-center the resting ball is hit, the greater the angle it will travel.

further Challenge

If you can get some heavy metal balls, you can make a record of how the balls travel when they collide. Place a piece of white paper on the floor, then put carbon paper on top of it. The pathway of the balls will be traced on the paper.

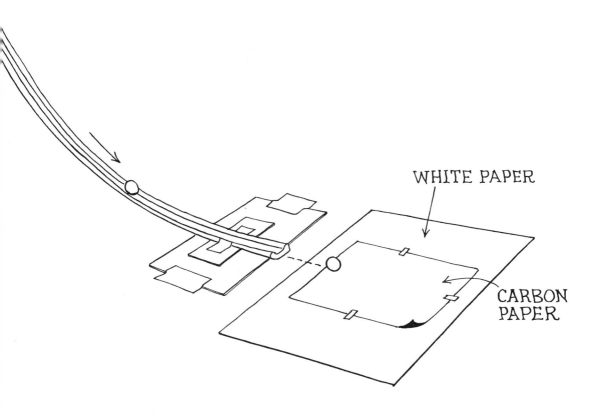

WHITE PAPER

CARBON PAPER

- Try hitting the ball at different angles, and after each try, record on the paper the position of the track in relation to the sitting ball. Can you predict ahead of time what these pathways will look like?

MORE COLLISIONS

If you place several identical balls at the bottom of a Big U track (see page 38) and roll a ball into them, strange things happen. This is fun to watch, and you can do some interesting experiments, too.

HOW MANY?

PLACE A PIECE OF
CARDBOARD HERE T
PREVENT BALLS FRO
JUMPING OFF WHEN H

Games and Experiments to Try

- What happens when you roll one ball into a group of six sitting ones?
- What happens when you roll two, three, or four balls into the six sitting ones?
- What happens if you roll a wooden or a plastic bead, a small rubber ball, or a cork ball into the group?

What's Happening?

When the rolling ball collides with the sitting ones, all of its energy and momentum is transferred to them. One ball colliding with the group results in the last ball in the row flying off the other end with the energy and momentum of the first ball. Two balls colliding with the group will result in two balls rolling off the other end. If one heavy ball hits the group, several balls will roll off the other end. The number of balls that fly off depend on the weight and speed of the rolling ball because, in this situation, the energy and momentum are not transferred in the same way.

Further Challenge

To compare how much energy is transferred when balls collide, set up the track as shown in the drawing below. Put a cork or a small can at the bottom of the Big U.

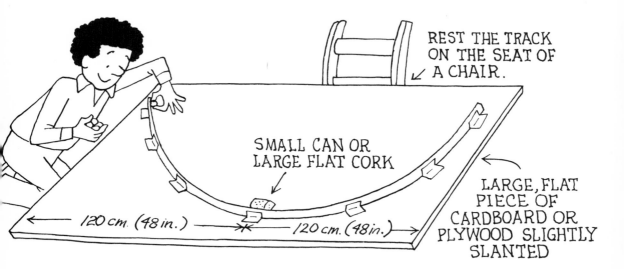

REST THE TRACK ON THE SEAT OF A CHAIR.

SMALL CAN OR LARGE FLAT CORK

LARGE, FLAT PIECE OF CARDBOARD OR PLYWOOD SLIGHTLY SLANTED

120 cm. (48 in.)

120 cm. (48 in.)

Roll a marble down the track and let it collide with the can or cork.

- How far will the cork move up the other side when it is hit by one marble? Mark on the cardboard where the cork was pushed.
- Will two or three marbles all rolled at the same time push the cork two or three times higher?
- What happens when a heavy ball such as a ball bearing collides with the cork?
- Try other kinds of balls and guess what will happen before you roll them. Each time, mark how high the cork was pushed.

Rube Goldberg Machines

Rube Goldberg was a very popular cartoonist who drew
pictures of complicated contraptions. Usually these were a
series of devices that were set off one after another. For
instance, instead of an ordinary alarm clock, he would create
a situation in which the sound of a crowing rooster would
disturb a dog that would wag its tail; the tail would trip a
lever that would start a ball rolling, which would cause a
weight to be pulled to the ceiling. When it reached the
ceiling, the weight would fall, hitting a bellows; the bellows
would blow on some feathers; the feathers would be near the
nose of the sleeping man, tickle his face, and wake him up.

In this section, you will find suggestions for making some
Rube Goldberg-type machines.

In all of the games so far, the ball only performed one kind
of action. In this section, you will have the ball do several
kinds of actions as it rolls down a track or a series of tracks.

In all the previous games, too, the ball only produced one
kind of action, although it could have done more. Remember,
you saw from the last two games that the moving ball had
energy and momentum that were transferred to other balls.
You can use this force and momentum and have the ball roll
through an obstacle course creating all kinds of effects. This
can be done by combining some or all of the previous games.

Here is one way you can put together some of the other games in the book to create a more complex, Rube Goldberg-type track. (This is only a suggestion and does not have to be followed exactly.)

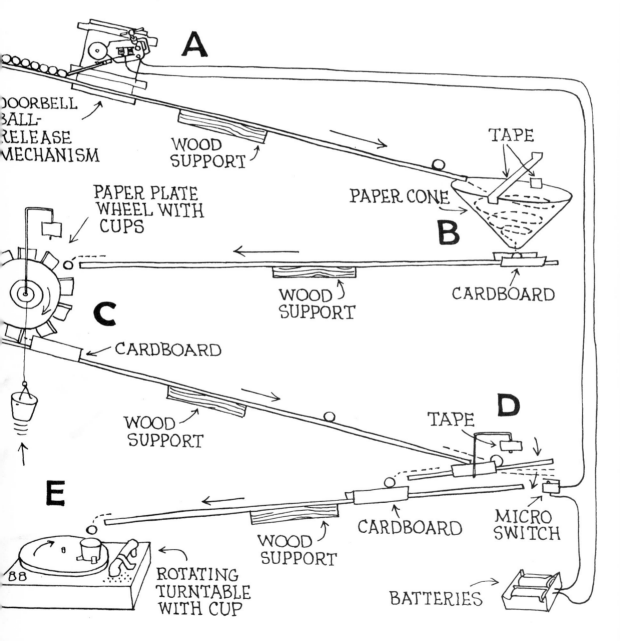

A

DOORBELL
BALL-
RELEASE
MECHANISM

WOOD
SUPPORT

TAPE

PAPER CONE

B

PAPER PLATE
WHEEL WITH
CUPS

C

WOOD
SUPPORT

CARDBOARD

CARDBOARD

WOOD
SUPPORT

TAPE

D

E

WOOD
SUPPORT

CARDBOARD

MICRO
SWITCH

ROTATING
TURNTABLE
WITH CUP

BATTERIES

This arrangement is a combination of several devices you have already seen, plus one new one. In assembling a contraption like this you need to proceed step by step.

First, find a wall or a large piece of cardboard that you can stick tape on. It should be flat and without bumps because you want the tracks straight. Start as high as you can. The higher you begin, the more devices you can add to your track. Next, assemble the tracks one at a time, as follows:

Step 1. Device *A*, is the same as the one on page 12.

Step 2. The second, *B*, is a paper cone. Its construction is shown on page 50. (Make sure to leave an opening at the bottom of the cone big enough for the ball to roll through.) Tape the outer and inner sides to the wall so the device is secure. You will have to make some positioning adjustments so that the ball rolls onto the cone and stays inside it. You may also need to tape a small piece of bent cardboard to the bottom of the cone to direct the ball onto the next track. Also tape a piece of cardboard to the track beneath the cone, as you did for the games on page 54, to make sure the ball rolls onto the next track without falling off.

Step 3. The wheel device, *C*, can be assembled as follows.

You will need:
>   4 paper plates
>   10 paper cups (3-oz. size)
>   masking tape
>   1 margarine cup and 2 margarine cup lids
>   ball-point pen tube
>   string
>   piece of wire hanger or any sturdy wire

To make the wheel device:

a. Find the center of the four plates and punch a hole through all of them.

b. Stick 9 or 10 paper cups to a strip of masking tape.

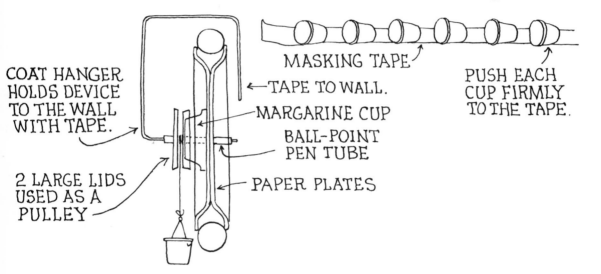

COAT HANGER
HOLDS DEVICE
TO THE WALL
WITH TAPE.

MASKING TAPE

←TAPE TO WALL.

—MARGARINE CUP

BALL–POINT
PEN TUBE

PUSH EACH
CUP FIRMLY
TO THE TAPE.

2 LARGE LIDS
USED AS A
PULLEY

← PAPER PLATES

c. Wrap this strip around the edge of the plates and secure it by taping down two or three cups to the plates. The cups should be evenly spaced around the wheel. You will have to experiment to find out how far apart they should be placed.

d. Punch holes in the center of the cup and lids.

e. Push the ball-point pen tube through everything.

f. Tape one end of the string inside the two lids.

g. Attach a cup to the other end of the string.

h. Attach the device to the wall by inserting a sturdy piece of wire through the ball-point pen tube. Tape the wire to the wall. Experiment to find out exactly where the wheel device should be placed in relation to the track in order to catch the ball and raise the cup on the string.

Step 4. The fourth device, *D*, is similar in construction to the one on page 31. Tape several nails to the end of the seesaw track as a counterweight to bring the track back once the ball rolls onto it. There should be just enough weight to make the other end hang above the micro switch.

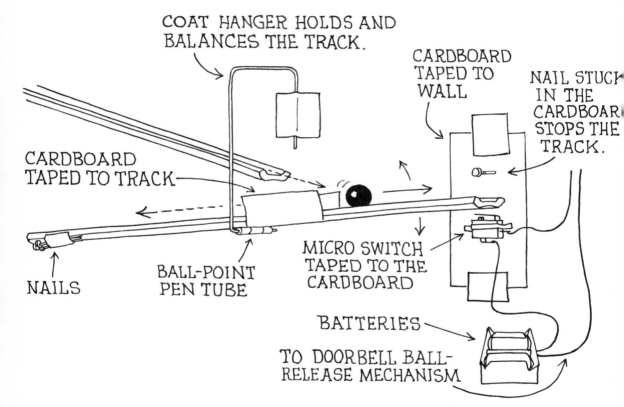

COAT HANGER HOLDS AND BALANCES THE TRACK.

CARDBOARD TAPED TO WALL

NAIL STUCK IN THE CARDBOARD STOPS THE TRACK.

CARDBOARD TAPED TO TRACK

NAILS

BALL-POINT PEN TUBE

MICRO SWITCH TAPED TO THE CARDBOARD

BATTERIES

TO DOORBELL BALL-RELEASE MECHANISM

When a ball rolls on the suspended track, it pushes down the track, which hits the micro switch, which in turn triggers the doorbell ball-release mechanism to release another ball at the top of the first track. Meanwhile, the first ball continues to roll down the suspended track onto the next section.

Step 5. The final device, *E*, is a record player with a cup taped to a rotating turntable, as on page 24. Before turning on the record player, position the cup near the end of the track so that the ball will fall into it. If the cup on the record player is not close enough to the wall for the ball to drop into it, tape a small piece of bent cardboard to the end of the track to direct the ball toward the cup.

SPIRAL BALL RETURN

With this device you can have a ball return to the starting point all by itself.

You will need:

> large dowel, about 120 cm. (4 ft.) long by 2 cm. ($\frac{3}{4}$ in.) in diameter (this can be purchased at hardware stores or lumberyards)
>
> clothesline rope (the amount you need will depend on the thickness of the rope)
>
> 1 margarine cup lid
>
> piece of cardboard
>
> record player
>
> masking tape
>
> 4 nails
>
> 2 pieces of molding, each 120 cm. (4 ft.) long
>
> wooden board, about 120 cm. (4 ft.) long

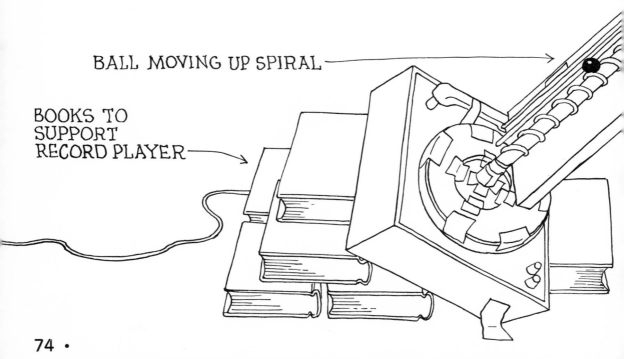

BALL MOVING UP SPIRAL

BOOKS TO SUPPORT RECORD PLAYER

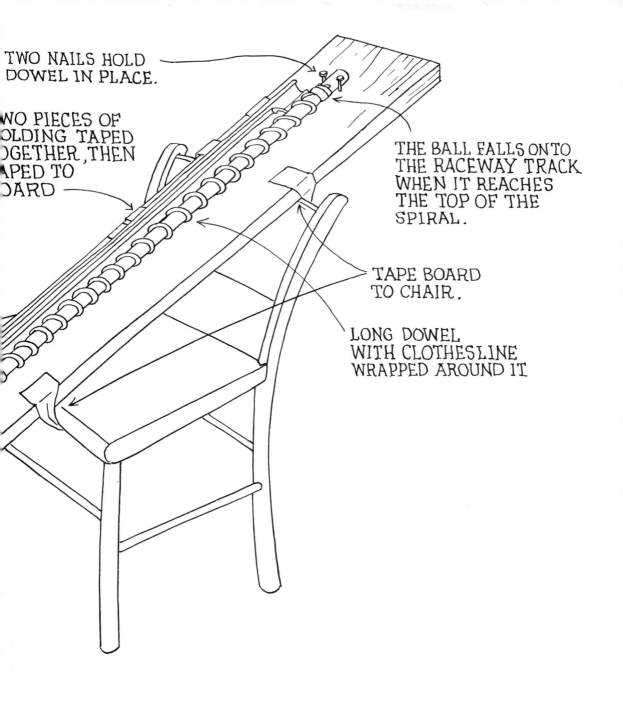

TWO NAILS HOLD
DOWEL IN PLACE.

[TW]O PIECES OF
[M]OLDING TAPED
[T]OGETHER, THEN
[T]APED TO
[B]OARD

THE BALL FALLS ONTO
THE RACEWAY TRACK
WHEN IT REACHES
THE TOP OF THE
SPIRAL.

TAPE BOARD
TO CHAIR.

LONG DOWEL
WITH CLOTHESLINE
WRAPPED AROUND IT

Step 1. To make the spiral, wrap the clothesline rope around the dowel as shown below. Tape the ends so they won't unravel.

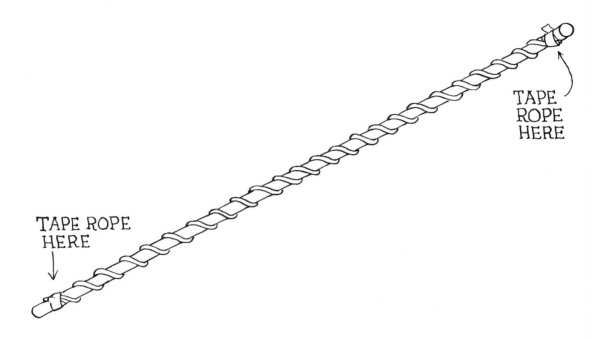

TAPE
ROPE
HERE

TAPE ROPE
HERE

Step 2. Make a small hole in one end of the dowel large enough so that it will fit on the record spindle in the middle of the turntable.

Step 3. Make a similar-sized hole in the center of the margarine cup lid.

Step 4. Cut out a circle from the cardboard so that it fits on top of the turntable.

Step 5. Center the plastic lid on the cardboard circle and trace around the lid. Cut out this portion from the cardboard and discard it.

Step 6. Tape the other, larger cardboard circle to the turntable.

Step 7. Tape the margarine cup lid to the end of the dowel, making sure you line up the holes.

Step 8. Push two nails through the lid. They should come through right next to the dowel, one on either side of it. Tape the nails to the dowel.

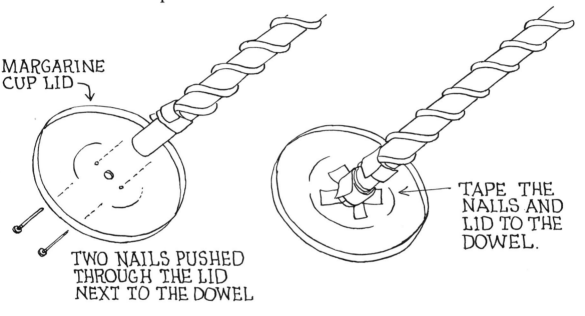

MARGARINE CUP LID

TWO NAILS PUSHED THROUGH THE LID NEXT TO THE DOWEL

TAPE THE NAILS AND LID TO THE DOWEL.

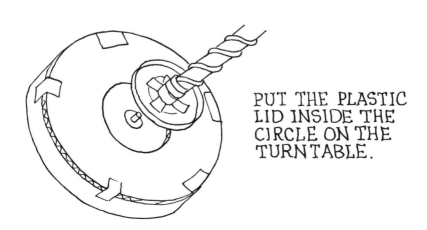

PUT THE PLASTIC LID INSIDE THE CIRCLE ON THE TURNTABLE.

Step 9. Put the plastic lid inside the cardboard circle on the turntable. It should fit tightly, and the record spindle should fit inside the holes in the lid and dowel. Tape the lid to the cardboard circle.

Step 10. Cut one end of a piece of molding at an angle. This piece will be used for the spiral. The cut angle should be at the top of the spiral device.

Step 11. Tape the two pieces of molding together as shown.

TAPE

TWO PIECES OF MOLDING

Step 12. Tape the board to a chair. Make sure the board is not resting on the record player or the turntable will not spin. Put the two pieces of molding on the board, tape them down, then place the spiral next to the molding. When everything is in place on the board, it should look like this:

ROPE

DOWEL

TAPE

THE BALL SITS BETWE
THE SPIRAL AND ONE (
THE MOLDINGS.

Step 13. To hold the top of the spiral in place, hammer a nail into the board on each side of the dowel. When you turn on the record player, the rope should move smoothly over the molding. The molding used for the spiral device should be slanted slightly away from the dowel so that the ball can be pushed up the track. You will have to adjust the angle of this slant so that the ball doesn't slip as it moves up the spiral.

As the spiral turns, it should push the ball to the top. The angle you cut in one of the pieces of molding will allow it to fall onto the raceway track positioned next to the spiral.

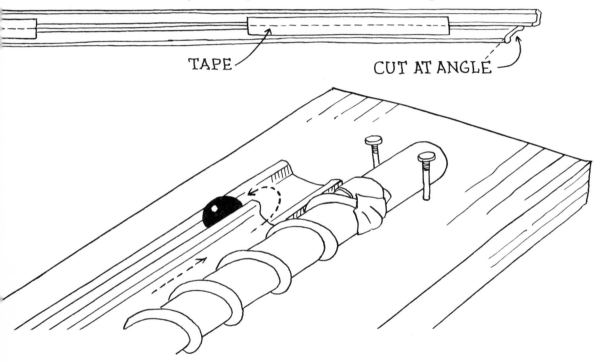

TAPE   CUT AT ANGLE

At first you can retrieve the ball as it reaches the end of the raceway track and place it back on the spiral yourself. Eventually, you can try to have the end of the raceway track deposit the ball at the bottom of the spiral so that it can start over again automatically.

CONTINUING CHALLENGES

The games described in this book are only some of the many you can create with the molding and balls. For instance, you could try to make the balls travel in spirals just as cars move down ramps in some parking garages. Or you can invent more games where balls crash into each other in different ways.

No matter what kind of game you create, watch carefully, and always experiment to see if you can better understand what is happening.